Bishop Robert J. Hermann's Homilies

Come Alive in Jesus!

Solemn Novena to
Our Lady of Mount Carmel
July 13-21, 2019

En Route Books & Media, LLC
St. Louis, MO

⊛*ENROUTE*
Make the time

En Route Books and Media, LLC
5705 Rhodes Avenue
St. Louis, MO 63109

Cover credit: Bev Wilson and TJ Burdick

Library of Congress Control Number: 2019950542

ISBN-13: 978-1-950108-50-3
ISBN-10: 1-950108-50-3

Come Alive in Jesus!

Bishop Robert J. Hermann

Auxiliary Bishop Emeritus

In gratitude to the

Carmelite Monastery of St. Joseph

Imprimatur: In accordance with CIC 827, permission to publish has been
granted on August 20, 2019 by the Most Reverend Mark S. Rivituso, D.D.,
J.C.L., Auxiliary Bishop, Archdiocese of St. Louis, Missouri. Permission to
publish is an indication that nothing contrary to Church teaching is contained in
this work. It does not imply any endorsement of the opinions expressed in the
publication; nor is any liability assumed by this permission

Chapter 1   God's Call to Holiness   Page 1

Chapter 2   The Need for Inner Quiet   Page 7

Chapter 3   Unilateral Forgiveness   Page 13

Chapter 4   Invoking Our Lady of Mount Carmel Page 19

Chapter 5   Spiritual Warfare   Page 25

Chapter 6   From Self-Hatred to God Reliance   Page 32

Chapter 7   Breaking into Heavenly Praise   Page 39

Chapter 8   Sacrament of the Present Moment   Page 47

Chapter 9   Abundant Weakness – Becoming
             Pregnant with God's Word   Page 54

Chapter One

God's Call to Holiness

Welcome to this first night of this Carmelite Novena, which lasts for nine nights.

We begin this first night by focusing on God's Call to Holiness – His mysterious call to each of us.

The whole novena is about imitating Mary in allowing God to enrich the love affair He has with us.

The nights at this novena may be hot, but not as hot as if we miss out on the kingdom, so in that sense this Novena is a cool place to be!

Besides, if any of you feel hot, perhaps you are not as hot in your garments as our priests are in their Mass vestments!

First of all, I want to express our collective gratitude to our Carmelite Sisters for making these sacred grounds available to us, not only for this novena but also for every day of the year.

A word about Carmel. Fr. Wilfrid McGreal tells us: "The Carmelite tradition speaks to those who long to be apart, to separate from smothering existence. The tradition offers the lure of wilderness, mountain retreat, vast expanses of desert. In solitude, a place apart, we searchers hope to hear our heart's desire more clearly, to reassess life, to dream, to be nourished by hidden springs, to meet the One whom others speak of with great assurance."

I follow up with a quote from Father John Welch, who in his book THE CARMELITE WAY, tells us:

"Carmel learned to tell the story of the human heart as a love story. Thinking they were searching for something missing in their lives, Carmelites discovered that they were being pursued by a loving Presence whose desire for them gave them increased life, greater freedom, and a trustworthy relationship for their guidance."

Notice what he in effect is saying: "As we search for something missing in our lives, we discover that we are being pursued by a loving Presence whose desire for us gives us increased life, greater freedom and a trustworthy relationship for our guidance."

This novena is all about God's call to holiness, and how our life is a response to His call.

The early Carmelites who gathered on Mount Carmel chose Mary to be their mother and their model. She is the one who taught them, and is teaching us, how to "Let it be done to us according to God's word." She taught them and us how to treasure God's word in our hearts. She taught them and us to "Do whatever He tells you."

To help you to understand your call to holiness, I want to begin with Jesus' call of Matthew as a tax collector. Remember, it was He who called you here tonight, and you are here to explore in your heart what this calling really means – a call to a deeper freedom and joy!

Let us begin with the Gospel of Matthew, Chapter 9:9.

"As Jesus passed on from there, he saw a man named Matthew sitting at the customs post. He said to him, 'Follow me.' And he got up and followed him."

To enter more fully into the call of Matthew, and of Christ's call to you and me, I want to share some of the brilliant and heartwarming insights of Brother Simeon, who wrote a three-volume commentary on the Gospel of Matthew.

Brother Simeon points out that Jesus' passing by and glancing at Matthew was not a casual passing by. He states that the Book of Wisdom tells us: "Wisdom, while remaining within itself, renews all things... and produces friends of God and prophets." (Wisdom 7:26ff)

That glance of Jesus was the power of God piercing the soul of Matthew. The glance of Jesus that brought you here tonight is the power of God entering your life in a deeper way!

He goes on to say: "The Savior erupts onto our lives at right angles to our horizontality – our all too flat and narrow 'horizon'. All of our hope resides in the fact that he sees us before we see him; his gaze penetrates our being before we have even formulated an imploration."

As it is, he goes on to say: "If grace reaches our heart, we will finally look up to Jesus and meet his eyes, but only stimulated by our sense of being fixed by someone's regard, of feeling the warmth of that gaze melting away our indifference and extricating us from our immersion in the ephemeral."

That is truly a mouthful, but a mouthful of delicious food to chew and digest!

"We cling to the petty lives we have constructed for ourselves just as surely as this man considers his existence inseparable from the tax collector's table, or as the paralytic looked upon his pallet as almost a part of his own anatomy. Ignorance becomes routine addiction to ambition or misery, and misery and ambition become… ourselves!

"The glance of Jesus descends… like a laser ray to restore us to freedom, to cut from our life the illusion of endless dependencies that we allow to suck away the substance of our person like so many leeches."

Before we take a closer look at how the glance of Jesus has affected and continues to affect our lives, let us take a look at the result of Jesus' loving glance at Matthew.

Matthew went from extorting money from people as a tax collector, to giving people the gospel as an evangelist. He gave the world 28 chapters of Gospel to replace the bad news he was inflicting on people. He added 68 pages to the Bible.

Not bad for a loving glance of Jesus!

If God did that to a tax collector, think of what he can do to our hearts!

His loving glance "renews all things and produces friends of God and prophets."

Christ's vertical entry into your heart forever changed your gaze. Before His entry you were horizontally fixated, unaware that there was a God above you who loved you.

He who first loved you gave you an inclination for a peace and freedom you did not know existed. It opened your heart to a longing for a deeper meaning in life. As Brother Simeon would say, His warm gaze into our soul began to melt away our indifference and it began freeing us from our immersion in the ephemeral.

Is it not true that when we listen to the evening news we feel a number of disturbances within, but when we spend quiet time reflecting on God's word, we feel a deep and abiding peace?

Brother Simeon says that we cling to the petty lives we have constructed for ourselves. It is here that "ignorance becomes routine addiction to ambition or misery, and misery becomes... ourselves!"

This is what the loving glance of Jesus does for us!

It is in quiet time that He offers us the image of ourselves as being beloved daughters or sons of the Father. It is in quiet time that the self-hatred and self-condemnation that often plague us disappear, and are replaced by joy and freedom.

It is in quiet prayer that we experience being pursued by a loving presence that gives us increased life, greater freedom and a trustworthy relation with our Savior.

In all of this, Our Mother of Mount Carmel is our model. It was she who always treasured God's word in her heart. It was that word that enabled her to say in all circumstances, "Let it be done to me according to thy word."

In the following evenings we will explore the power of inner silence, how to rise above those inner voices which rob us of so much peace, how to unilaterally forgive others, how to deal decisively with all issues of spiritual warfare and come into a new freedom.

We will deal clearly with how to overcome self-hatred and self-condemnation and become the beloved children of God we are called to be.

We will explore how to join Mary in Magnifying the Lord and entering more deeply into praise and joy.

These are some of the steps the Lord is offering us so that we can experience in a deeper way the fruit of His personal call to each of us.

May we ask Our Lady of Mount Carmel for the grace to quietly contemplate God's word in our hearts, and then to embrace His will each day as it comes along.

Mary, Our Lady of Mount Carmel, pray for us.

Chapter Two

Need for Inner Quiet

Today is the second day of our novena. Yesterday we focused on the call to holiness and how Jesus' loving glance at Matthew enabled him to come apart from the world and follow Jesus.

Today we will focus on the need for inner quiet to hear the word of God.

In the gospel we have a lawyer trying to trap Jesus, and Jesus turns the table on the lawyer by asking him what God's law about entering the kingdom of heaven is all about. The lawyer replies:

"You shall love the Lord your God with all of your heart, with all of your soul, with all of your strength, and with all of your mind; and your neighbor as yourself."

In his head the lawyer knows what these commandments mean, but he is looking for Jesus to give him some consolation by saying: "Good job! Keep it up!" He doesn't get that from Jesus, so he asks Him: "Who is my neighbor?"

Jesus then relates to him the story of the person who fell victim to robbers. The priest and the Levite saw him but passed him by. The Good Samaritan, on the other hand, stopped by, poured oil into his sores and bandaged him up, took him to an inn keeper and gave him money to take care of him, with a promise to pay more if needed.

Why did the Levite and the priest pass him by? In their head they knew God's law of hospitality, but they were ruled by their egotistical inner noises. They didn't want to be bothered by this inconvenience.

In addition, they did not want to render themselves ritually unclean. They were driven by the voices of selfish interests.

It is very obvious that the law of God's love never captured their hearts. It stayed in their heads. In their present focus of mind, this individual's plight had no connection with their relationship with God. In other words, did these two individuals pray at all? If their life came to a sudden end, where would their souls go?

On the other hand, the Samaritan, who did take care of the victim, belonged to a nation of people hated by the Jews. The Samaritans were certainly not welcome to worship in the temple in Jerusalem.

Yet, this Samaritan represents the heavenly qualities of compassion, healing and love. The story shows that God's goodness was living in the heart of the Samaritan and that the victim's plight was an opportunity for godly virtues to flow forth from his heart.

In other words, he had an inner quiet, and God's word was alive in his heart. Without a doubt, this Samaritan spent quality time in daily prayer, and God's values were alive in his heart.

If you and I had suddenly come upon this victim of robbers, how would we have come off? Would we have looked around to see if anyone was looking? Never mind that God is always looking, even though we trust he will keep quiet about it if we fail – yet our betrayal of our God will hound us in our consciences!

Are there times in the day when we erupt with anger or irritation when someone does or says something offensive to us? Worse yet, do we react with resentment, but hide it from others and attempt to deny it ourselves?

How would you and I feel if God handed out a printout of our hidden thoughts and compulsions? What if he had them posted on Facebook?

All of us, without exception, have unredeemed compulsions just below the surface of our awareness. They often surface in stress.

We were all created with human limitations, and God loves us in our limitations. However, He is calling us to turn to Him in our weaknesses.

This is why daily quiet time reflecting on His word is so vitally important if we are to seek help with our unredeemed within.

"The word of God is keener than a two-edged sword. It is able to pierce between bone and marrow and lay bare the thoughts of men." Jesus said: "The truth shall set you free!" Again, the psalmist tells us: "Be still and know that I am God."

When we take our compulsions to quiet prayer and reflect on God's word, we sit there with the unpleasantness of our volatile compulsions confronted by the truth of God's word. As we stay in silence, gradually the unpleasantness of our unruly compulsions retreats and is replaced by a quiet peace.

This is the quiet with which we are invited to begin each day. Quiet prayer always quells the unruly compulsions that are ready to erupt at any moment.

As one person commented, "Daily we wake up to the rebellions ready to erupt!"

Recently, when I awoke, I quickly surveyed the day's work ahead, and realized that it went late into the evening. I was tired and said to myself: "How will I have enough energy to do all the work I am asked to do today?"

Then thought of the coming morning meditation came and I just smiled away the concern, and was filled with peace.

Quiet time makes us stouthearted in the Lord!

Cardinal Sarah tells us in his book *The Power of Silence*: "Silence is difficult, but it makes man able to allow himself to be led by God. Silence is born of silence. Through God, the silent one, we can gain access to silence. And man is unceasingly surprised by the light that bursts forth then."

"Silence is more important than any other human work. For it expresses God. The true revolution comes from silence; it leads us toward God and others so as to place ourselves humbly and generously at their service." (p. 68)

St. John of the Cross tells us in his work, *The Ascent of Mount Carmel*, that the journey to God begins with a downward descent through death of self. Christ could not ascend to God without first dying.

Our inner nature, un-redeemed as it is, cannot ascend to God without first dying to its attachments.

Silent time allows our un-redeemed compulsions to rise into consciousness so that we can invite the Lord to enter into these compulsions and bring into them freedom and healing.

I once remember a parishioner saying to me: "We should not have silent time after communion because that is such a negative experience."

An infection on the body needs to be lanced so that its poisons can be released from the body. It is then that the healing properties of the body can go to work and bring complete restoration. This is what happens when we enter into silence. We allow Jesus to lance our wound with His word, and to simultaneously heal it with His love.

Silent time is such a rich experience of being loved by Jesus in the midst of our weaknesses. If we stay with silence, knowing that Jesus is presiding, we are filled with peace because He is bringing healing into the depths of our soul.

If you have a fear of silence, ask Jesus to help you enter into what it is that He wants to do in your heart.

Carve out a time of daily silence and allow Jesus to take over.

In subsequent nights we will explore how to rise above those inner voices which rob us of so much peace, how to unilaterally forgive others, how to deal decisively with all issues of spiritual warfare and thus come into a new freedom. We will also explore how to overcome issues of self-hatred and self-condemnation and experience what it is like to be a beloved child of our Heavenly Father.

We will explore how to join Mary in Magnifying the Lord and entering more deeply into praise and joy.

These are some of the steps Our Lord is offering us so that we can experience in a deeper way the fruit of his personal call to each of us. Let us continue to ask Our Lady of Mount Carmel to lead us to a greater intimacy with Jesus.

Psalm 46 tells us: "Be Still and Know that I Am God!"

Mary, Our Lady of Mount Carmel, pray for us.

Chapter Three

Unilateral Forgiveness

Today is the third day of our Novena. On the first day we focused on the call to holiness. Yesterday we focused on the need for inner quiet so as to be able to hear the word of God.

Today I will focus upon Unilateral Forgiveness.

St. John of the Cross teaches us that one of the dominant reasons for a lack of inner quiet stems from an inordinate attachment to a perceived good, apart from its relationship to God.

In the two great commandments, God teaches us to love Him above all things and our neighbor as ourselves.

In the Lord's Prayer, we ask our Heavenly Father to forgive us our trespasses as we forgive those who trespass against us.

This flows from the simple command that we are to love others as we love ourselves and to forgive others as we desire that they forgive us. Hence, when we refuse to forgive others, or when we put all sorts of conditions on our extending forgiveness, then we are clearly attached to our own will and not to God's will.

We find it especially difficult to forgive others unless we receive from them an apology or reassurance that they will never offend us again.

Tonight, I want to share with you a gift that cuts through all that attachment to self-will. This gift is called "Unilateral Forgiveness." It simply means that we extend forgiveness to others without any reassurances on their part.

In my life I experienced a marvelous breakthrough by listening to a teaching entitled "Unilateral Forgiveness" by a very holy Lutheran pastor named Larry Christiansen. This teaching is so powerful that we have given away over two thousand copies over the past thirty years, with the author's permission.

In this teaching on Unilateral Forgiveness, Pastor Christensen points out that sometimes we withhold forgiveness from others until they come back and apologize, but they are so bound down in their sins that they can't apologize.

Nowhere in the gospels, perhaps with the exception of the Good Thief, does anyone ask Jesus for forgiveness. They are bound down in their sins and cannot ask. Jesus extended forgiveness to them where they were.

Zacchaeus did not ask for forgiveness. Jesus invited Himself to lunch in Zacchaeus' home so they could talk things over. Jesus said to him: "Today salvation has come to this house because this man too is a descendant of Abraham."

In the case of the lame man, as well as the case of the paralytic, Jesus simply said: "Your sins are forgiven."

In the case of the Samaritan woman, Jesus opened a conversation with a woman who was married and divorced five times and now was living with another man outside of marriage.

By the time Jesus finished his dialogue, He reconciled her with her fellow Samaritans who previously hated her, and then she went out and invited them to meet Jesus, the Messiah. When these Samaritans found Jesus, they begged Him to stay with them for two days!

Jesus made a lot of friends with the Father by simply inviting sinners to repentance.

In listening to this teaching on Unilateral Forgiveness, I realized that one individual who had hurt me and whom I found it so hard to forgive, was apparently bound down in his sins and could not come to me and ask me for forgiveness, but I could extend forgiveness to him wherever he was!

To me this was a very eye-opening experience. I did not even have to give him a call. I could just beam out Christ's forgiveness as a radio station beams out its radio waves.

I simply interpreted the teaching on Unilateral Forgiveness to extend forgiveness to anyone and everyone who had hurt me.

This was a very freeing experience. A lot of oppression left me that day. That day I learned a lot about spiritual warfare, and tomorrow we will get into that.

This one person in particular I found hard to forgive because of repeated offenses, but I not only forgave him, but I also asked Jesus to bless him where he was and to help him in his relationship with Jesus and with the persons with whom he lived and worked.

To my surprise, two days later he came back and apologized. (At the time I did not know that he was struggling with chemical addiction.)

One month later he called me on the phone and asked me to meet with him for the Baptism of the Holy Spirit. What an incredible joy that was.

Unilateral Forgiveness – what a gift that is! We do not have to call people on the phone and offer it to them. In fact, they may have forgotten it and become very insulted that we were bringing up the issue.

We need simply to come before Jesus and join Him in extending His forgiveness to them. The divine wireless Internet was with us long before the age of electronics!

Just think of all the blessings you can send out by extending Unilateral Forgiveness to anyone who has ever hurt you. Make sure you put your whole heart into it! You do not have to contact them by phone. Jesus will take care of that for you. When you extend that forgiveness, the results are often instantaneous!

I know that you may find it difficult to take this step. This is where Our Lady of Mount Carmel comes in. She has been mother to the Carmelite family for many centuries! You can only imagine the number of disagreements over the centuries that threatened to rupture community living. Without her constant intercession, they would never have remained a family.

Let Mary be your intercessor as she was theirs! Time and time again she interceded for them individually and collectively as they reached impasses in their relationships.

Remember at the Wedding Feast of Cana she said to Jesus: "Son, they have no more wine!"

Then she said to the stewards: "Do whatever He tells you." We all know the results.

Mary stood by the Cross when Jesus said: "Father, forgive them for they know not what they do!"

As you allow Mary to intercede for you, may she hear you say: "Jesus, forgive this person without any preconditions or strings attached. Not only forgive them but also bless them so that they may feel good about themselves and their relationship with others and with their God." Every time you think of them, renew this powerful prayer. Mary will help you bring it to completion so that even negative feelings and memories will disappear.

I have not found any other teaching that has as dramatic effects as Unilateral Forgiveness! As you live and practice this, you will bring great joy to Jesus and Mary, as well as to those whom you forgive without any reservations.

Another reason that Unilateral Forgiveness is so powerful is that it is such an effective weapon against spiritual warfare. Tomorrow night, we will celebrate the great feast of Our Lady of Mount Carmel. On Wednesday, we will deal with spiritual warfare. On following nights, we will allow our Lady to model for us how to magnify the Lord, as well as how to treasure God's word in our hearts so that it can become flesh within us.

Mary, Our Lady of Mount Carmel, pray for us.

Chapter Four

Feast of Our Lady of Mount Carmel

Today we celebrate the Feast of Our Lady of Mount Carmel.

According to the traditions of the Carmelite order, on this day, July 16, in 1251, the Blessed Virgin Mary appeared to St. Simon Stock, a Carmelite, and revealed to him the Scapular of Our Lady of Mount Carmel.

Wearing the Brown Scapular is in a sense putting on the clothing of Mary, her contemplative prayer life, her continual embracing of God's will for Her, and Her desire to help others come to know Jesus.

When the founding monks first gathered together on Mount Carmel to begin a monastic community, they knew that they needed all the help and guidance they could get, so they chose Mary, the Mother of God to be their Mother and their model. They built a chapel on Mount Carmel and named it Our Lady of Mount Carmel.

They realized that already at the Annunciation when Mary said to the angel: "Let it be done to me according to thy word," Mary was the mother of mankind's savior and therefore in reality mankind's mother.

It was on the Cross that Jesus said to John and to us: "Son, behold your mother." At that moment, she officially became our mother.

These early Carmelites were also aware that Mary was with the Apostles in the upper room as well as at Pentecost. She was their consultant in the early days of evangelization.

These early Carmelites knew that they needed all the help they could get in learning how to live in community in love and to reach out to others in love.

To understand more clearly what is at the heart of Mount Carmel, let us review how Father John Welch summarized the story of Carmel:

"Carmel learned to tell the story of the human heart as a love story. Thinking they were searching for something missing in their lives, Carmelites discovered that they were being pursued by a loving Presence whose desire for them gave them increased life, greater freedom and a trustworthy relationship for their guidance."

Carmel becomes a love story because they looked to Mary for guidance in how to become evangelized and then how to share the gift of evangelization with others.

Mary was Jesus' first and prized disciple. She proclaimed her readiness to be evangelized at the moment of the Annunciation when she said: "Let it be done to me according to thy word."

She modeled for them how to form a community by allowing the Holy Spirit to form them and transform them from their individual selves into a community.

This requires inner change, which cannot be purchased on the open market, but can only be formed by the Holy Spirit, transforming the hearts of the monks who gathered together daily to reflect on the word of God.

"Let it be done to me according to thy word" was at the heart of each monk's daily prayer and activity. It was this prayer that also led him daily to submit his heart to the will of God as it was manifested to him in community.

As they began to see their individual hearts being converted and the early vestiges of community forming, they could rejoice with Our Lady at the Visitation: "My soul magnifies the Lord, and my spirit rejoices in God my Savior."

Just as Mary rejoiced in how God was calling her to be the mother of Our Savior, these early monks could rejoice at what God was doing in them, forming a community of faithful that would last for centuries and grow and eventually spread over the whole world.

I am certain that whenever individuals found the words of scripture especially challenging, Mary would remind them of what she told the stewards at Cana: "Do whatever He tells you!"

I am certain that whenever they obeyed Mary, they saw similar fruits, perhaps not a multiplication of the wine from the vine but an outpouring of the new wine, which always brought amazing results to the community.

Yes, Our Lady of Mount Carmel wants to do the same thing today for each of us.

Mary is modeling for us how to embrace God's will in our lives, even if we do not understand it. We are called to trust God in all circumstances, and God will fulfill our hearts' desires as we embrace His will in our lives, which includes embracing His cross as it comes to us. That is what Mary did in such an admirable way on Calvary.

When Mary visits Elizabeth, she "magnifies the Lord and rejoices in God [her] Savior." Mary recognizes that she is carrying in her womb the Savior of the world. She does not understand all of this, but she does recognize that through the Savior she is bearing, all the world will be blessed in every generation.

You and I are also called to magnify the Lord in all circumstances. Even when crosses come our way, if we embrace them and magnify the Lord even in suffering, then we are giving the Lord glory in rejoicing with Jesus within us that He who is mighty is doing great things within us and holy is His name.

Finally, we are to imitate Mary in her position of constant prayer before the throne of God.

How obvious it is today that the Church and the world need a fresh outpouring of the Holy Spirit. As we cry out for a fresh outpouring of the Holy Spirit, Mary is right there with us, encouraging us and modeling for us how to receive the gifts of the Holy Spirit.

Mary has demonstrated again and again how much she desires to encourage us to join her in praying for the conversion of sinners. We see this again in her appearances at Fatima where she invites us afresh to pray for the conversion of sinners.

When she appears at Fatima, she is holding in her right hand a scapular, as if to remind us once again to clothe ourselves in the values she lived and the values she continues to promote.

A number of years ago, a Carmelite monk visited Sr. Lucy in Fatima and asked her, "Some people say the Brown Scapular is more important than the Rosary and others say the opposite. Who is right?"

Sr. Lucy said: "Both are the same. Both are the clothing of Mary."

We conclude our remarks on this great feast day by asking you to listen carefully to the words of today's preface, the Preface of the Mother of Our Lady of Carmel.

"[Mary] shares with Christ his work of salvation and with his Church she brings forth sons and daughters whom she calls to walk the path of perfect love.

She claims us also as her beloved children, clothed in the habit of her Order, shields us along the way of holiness and in her likeness sets us before the world so that our hearts, like hers, may ever contemplate your word, love our brothers and sisters, and draw them to her Son."

Mary, Our Lady of Mount Carmel, pray for us.

Chapter Five

Spiritual Warfare

God is inviting all of us into the intimacy of the most Holy Trinity.

In following the general theme of the call to holiness and the obstacles that sometimes stand in our way, two days ago we focused on Unilateral Forgiveness as a way of breaking through some of the inner static that sometimes rules our lives.

Today we will focus on Spiritual Warfare, which is very closely related to Unilateral Forgiveness. Tomorrow we will focus on how to overcome negative patterns of thought in our lives.

To very briefly review: Unilateral forgiveness is simply extending God's forgiveness to others without their asking for it. They are bound down in their sins and cannot ask.

Today we are going to look at a deeper reason that binds them down. Once we understand this deeper reason, we have power to dramatically make a break-through into freedom.

One of the deeper reasons that bind people down in their sins is the invisible influence of evil spirits.

Paul tells us: "Be angry, but do not sin. Do not let the sun go down upon your anger so as to give Satan a foothold."

He also tells us: "Our warfare is not against flesh and blood, but against the principalities and powers of this world of darkness."

So many people are afflicted by badly strained relationships or broken relationships, and they have no idea that they are dealing with an evil spirit.

When we do not forgive but hold on to anger and un-forgiveness, we unknowingly invite in evil spirits that oppress us more and more.

Before we ago further, let us briefly establish the reality of Satan in our midst as we find this in Bible and in the teachings of the Church.

In Genesis 3:15 we see God addressing Satan in the serpent: "I will put enmity between you and the woman, between your offspring and hers; he will strike at your head while you strike at his heal."

In the Book of Revelation, we read: "Then war broke out in Heaven; Michael and his angels battled the dragon... The huge dragon, the ancient serpent, who is called the devil and Satan, who deceived the whole world, was thrown down to the earth, and his angels were thrown down with him."

This is what scripture tells us.

However, with the advent of the Vatican Council some scriptural scholars began to recast Jesus' ministry of exorcism as healing psychologically ill people. On several occasions Cardinal Ratzinger has taken to task those biblical exegetes who try to recast the exorcisms performed by Jesus as psychological healings. He said they have ignored the Fathers of the Church as well as Thomas Aquinas and his theology.

Vatican II tells us: "For a monumental struggle against the power of darkness pervades the whole history of man. The battle was joined from the very origins of the world and will continue until the last day as the Lord has attested. Caught in this conflict, man is obliged to wrestle constantly if he is to cling to what is good, nor can he achieve his own integrity without great efforts and the help of God's grace."

Pope Paul VI, in a General Audience in November 1973, tells us: "What are the greatest needs of the Church today? Do not let our answer surprise you as being over simple or even superstitious and unreal: one of the greatest needs is defense from the evil which we call the Devil."

He continues, "So we know that this dark and disturbing spirit really exists, and that he still acts with treacherous cunning; he is the secret enemy that sows errors and misfortunes in human history."

With that background, let us address tonight's topic of spiritual warfare.

In Ephesians Paul tells us: "Our warfare is not against flesh and blood but against the principalities and powers of this world of darkness." Again, he tells us: "Do not let the sun go down upon your anger so as to give Satan a foothold."

When we hold on to anger, resentment or un-forgiveness, the evil one can come in to set up shop, and usually does. When this happens, we are in need of deliverance, whether we know it or not.

Forty years ago, at a quiet 6:30 a.m. Mass I discovered what the deliverance ministry was all about. The Mass was suddenly interrupted with a blood-curdling shriek!

The eyes of the parishioners were on a person in the fourth pew. We were all frightened, so I went over and saw her praising God and crying at the same time. To calm all attendants, I led them in two stanzas of "Holy God We Praise Thy Name." Needless to say, we were all off key, but it worked!

In the sacristy after Mass, she was excited because after years of bitterness toward her alcoholic brother for pestering the neighbors for money, she was finally able to forgive him! She did not know that she let out a loud shriek when the evil spirits departed. She just received the gift of tongues for which she had been praying, but which was blocked because of bitterness, un-forgiveness, resentment and anger.

It was through the gift of repentance that she was released from this oppression.

Every Christian person has the right to command the evil one to leave his or her individual life. This power is part of the baptismal vows of renouncing Satan.

If you don't know who you are, you are afraid of Satan. If you realize that you are, through Baptism, a beloved son or daughter of the Father, a sister or brother of Jesus, and a temple of the Holy Spirit, Satan is afraid of you!

Genuine repentance of the sin is necessary for deliverance. Amos said: "Can two walk together unless they have agreed?"

When we continue to hold on to a sin, we are inviting Satan to come in and harass us.

Once one is genuinely sorry for the sin and repents, a good formula for the renunciation of the specific evil spirit is:

"In the name of Jesus Christ, I cancel all agreements with: (name the spirit or cluster of spirits) the spirit of anger, the spirit of resentment, the spirit of un-forgiveness, etc. and command them to go to the foot of the Cross and obey Jesus."

This is powerful, but it must be spoken from the heart with force and meaning.

While lay people are encouraged to take authority over the evil spirits oppressing themselves, they should not pray a prayer of command for the evil spirit to leave another person, but rather pray intercessory prayers, such as Hail Mary, Our Father or the St. Michael Prayer.

These are very powerful ways of assisting another person to experience complete deliverance.

Generally, the evil spirit responds to the name of the sin behind which it hides. With the sin of anger there may be a whole cluster of evil spirits, in addition to anger. These might include un-forgiveness, resentment, retaliation, bitterness, revenge, etc.

If the problem persists, then ask a priest to help with prayers of deliverance.

Since that time, I have seen hundreds of people set free from the bondage of the evil one. The two most common entry points for the evil one are sins of passion, such as lust and anger and their relatives, on the one hand, and sins of curiosity whereby individuals seek hidden knowledge from the evil one. The most common form of this latter is the Ouija board.

Spiritual warfare is also very much at work in the whole area of negativity, towards ourselves and towards others.

Jesus said: "The evil one has come to rob, to slaughter and to destroy. I have come that you might have life and have it more abundantly. I have come that you might have my joy and that your joy might be complete."

Tomorrow we will deal with how to get rid of the negativity in our lives, so that we can be the joyful persons we are called to be.

Meanwhile, continue to ask Mary to help you understand how to apply the word of God to your life, and continue practicing daily silent prayer as did the great Carmelite saints.

Mary, Our Lady of Mount Carmel, pray for us.

Chapter Six

From Self-Hatred to Christ Reliance

Brief review of topics:

1. Call to Holiness
2. Call to Inner Quiet
3. Unilateral Forgiveness
4. Invoking our Lady of Mount Carmel
5. Spiritual Warfare (when the Lord used a loud clap of thunder to punctuate our topic)
6. From Self-Hatred to Christ Reliance

I begin with a story. The parents of twins visited a psychologist with their dilemma. One of the twins was an incurable pessimist and other an unrealistic optimist.

They asked the psychologist for his help.

He told them to create two environments. In the first, place a large stack of gift-wrapped toys in a room with his name on each gift.

Then create a horse stable with a pile of horse manure in it and a pitchfork.

Place the pessimist into the room with all the toys and then observe him through a glass in the door. They did.

He just sat there, looking very glum. When the parents came in and said, "Why not unwrap the toys and play with them?" The boy said: "I am afraid I will break them."

They looked into the horse stable to observe the optimist. He was digging through the pile of horse manure with great gusto! When they asked him what he was doing, he said: "With this much horse manure there's got to be a pony somewhere!"

Psychologists can shed great light on the science of the mind, but only grace can heal the deep spiritual wounds of the heart.

We began this retreat by quoting Father John Welch as saying: "Carmel learned to tell the story of the human heart as a love story. Thinking they were searching for something missing in their lives, Carmelites discovered that they were being pursued by a loving Presence whose desire for them gave them increased life, greater freedom, and a trustworthy relationship for their guidance."

So, what are we really searching for?

So often, when we are first awakened to the spiritual journey within, we see the tremendous discrepancy between ourselves and our God and we make the mistake of taking charge of fixing ourselves to make ourselves more pleasing to God.

This is a disaster!

God created us to be dependent upon others and upon Him. He doesn't hate us when we sin. He sees our weaknesses as our potential excuse to welcome Him in to help us to develop a deeper relationship with Him.

Holy people are people poked full of holes so that God's mercy can get into them!

Because we cannot fix ourselves, our repeated efforts to make ourselves holy only lead us to incessant frustration, which leads to more anger, more resentment, more self-hatred and most dangerous of all, more self-condemnation.

Instead of turning to Jesus in our weaknesses and asking Jesus for mercy and thus coming into a new freedom, we turn against ourselves and refuse His offer. This is our downfall - not receiving His mercy, and thus not coming into a new freedom!

Eventually we end up angry at self, at others, and even at God Himself because He is not listening to our wonderful plan to make ourselves more loveable and more acceptable to Him!

Let me say a word about self-hatred and self-condemnation. When we enter into self-hatred, we are really blaspheming Jesus, because the Father looks down upon us and sees the great work His beloved Son is doing in us, and all we see is a spirit of self-hatred.

We don't see Jesus loving us and forgiving us! Instead, we allow the spirit of self-condemnation to come in and we agree with his condemnation rather than with Jesus' work of redeeming us. This is a huge mistake!

To confront this lie, we need to look at what Jesus tells us in the Gospel of John: "God sent his only begotten Son into the world, not to condemn the world, but to save it."

Because we have not turned to Jesus to ask for His mercy for our sins, we have chosen to agree with the evil one to condemn ourselves.

When we refuse to accept the mercy of Jesus for our sins, we turn away from Jesus to the evil one!

Jesus goes on to say: "Whoever believes in [Me] will not be condemned, but whoever does not believe has already been condemned, because he has not believed in the name of the only Son of God."

If I really believe and accept the forgiveness of Jesus, then I am really robbing Satan of his lies that I should condemn myself!

The truth that I need to hear is that by Baptism I have become a beloved child of the Father, the brother or sister of Jesus, and a temple of the Holy Spirit.

The truth is that God the Father spoke on Mount Tabor to Peter, James and John and said: "This is my beloved Son."

He was also saying to them that when they follow Jesus, they become beloved sons and daughters of the Father.

When the Father looks down upon us, He does not see our sins as much as He sees His Son alive in us, and He sees us as His beloved children.

In the Gospel of John at the Last Supper Jesus told His apostles: "As the Father has loved me, so I have loved you. Live on in my love."

When I ask Jesus: "Are you saying that you and the Father have been together for all eternity, and now when we whippersnappers come along you love us as much as the Father loves you?" Christ's answer is: "Of course."

Are you saying that the Father loves us as much as He loves you? Jesus response: "Most certainly."

I respond by saying, "Father, if that is the case, I really like Your attitude toward me much better than I like my attitude about myself. Would You help me download Your image of myself and help me to live in that image?"

God really wants to do this and now is able to do this because we have renounced the lie about condemnation and self-condemnation.

Now we are ready to embrace the Father's true image of ourselves. We no longer believe the lies of the evil spirit of condemnation.

Instead, we come before the Father and allow Him to shower us in His truth of who we are. His shower of truth bathes away the dark, condemning lies, and helps us to see ourselves as Our Father sees us. This brings the Father so much joy!

We need to take a spiritual daily shower, allowing the Holy Trinity to shower us with the mercy of Jesus, the Father's truth that we are His beloved children, and the love of the Holy Spirit, who enables us to love ourselves and to love others as ourselves.

It is most helpful to remember when a negative issue arrives, that we not get trapped in dealing with that one negative issue, but that we first refresh ourselves in the Father's true image of us, and let that true image guide us in the issue before us.

Let us use each issue that comes up as an opportunity to turn to the Father's image of who we are. This is a seminal stance we are invited to adopt.

This is a redeemed way of living. If our body needs a daily shower to keep it fresh, how much more does our spirit also need a daily shower of Trinitarian truth to live in the realization every day that we are beloved children of the Father?

When we live in the freshness of the Holy Trinity, we have new energy, we have joy, we have a life-giving relationship with the Holy Trinity!

So, if I were your spiritual physician, I would give you a daily prescription of taking a 15-minute shower of truth with the Most Holy Trinity as you begin each day.

The people with whom you live will readily notice the difference!

Mary, Our Lady of Mount Carmel, pray for us.

Chapter Seven

Breaking into Heavenly Praise

(Warming up for eternity!)

I begin with a story.

Julia was a sophomore in college, and her dad had very high expectations for her. In the second semester of her sophomore year she wrote the following letter:

"Dear Dad,

I can't tell you how happy I am since I met Ichabod at a drug clinic. We are expecting twins in the fall.

Every day I wake up I am so filled with joy and happiness. I just look forward to discovering something new each day."

She continues on the back page:

"Dad, there is no Ichabod in my life. I have not been in a drug clinic and I am not expecting. However, I did get a "D" in chemistry. Please keep things in perspective!

Signed: *Julia*

Tonight, I will explore with you how imitating Mary in praising God can help us keep things in perspective. (Perhaps that is how she dealt with Joseph's disappointment in not getting to marry her!)

Tonight, I want to focus on how to throw a really great party without any money - how to throw a praise party for our God. I want to explore the incredible power that praising God has to change our inner environment.

We can be so ticked off that smoke may be coming out of our ears, yet when we enter into praising God freely, the smoke all goes away and we are left wondering what just happened.

The answer is simple. We just entered into another world!

We begin with the Book of Daniel and the three men in the fiery furnace. They are having a ball in the midst of the fiery furnace praising God and singing at the top of their voices!

Listen to them praising God:

"Blessed are you, O Lord, the God of our ancestors, praiseworthy and exalted above all forever;"

"And blessed is your holy and glorious name, praiseworthy and exalted above all forever."

"For he has delivered us from Sheol and saved us from the power of death; He has freed us from the raging flame and delivered us from the fire."

They are having a ball, marching about in the midst of the flames, with praise as their asbestos suits, protecting them from the flames.

Before I get into the scriptures, which show us how praising God is a warmup for all eternity, I want to share with you how praise of God opened my eyes to have a ball of fun when everything was going wrong!

It all happened in the Fall of 1974. I was a full-time teacher at Prep North and was really looking forward to All Saints Day, when I was free to visit my parents.

Two days before, I found out that we were to have a Priest Council meeting at 1:00 p.m. that day.

O K, I would leave immediately after that.

When I arrived at the meeting the director of priest personnel said he wanted to meet with me immediately after the Priest Council meeting. He informed me I was being transferred. I told him I didn't want to be transferred, but he said that was beside the point.

So, I resigned myself to miss visiting my parents that day. It was a gloomy, dark, dank, foggy and drizzly day!

After that meeting, I decided I still wanted to do something worthwhile, so I decided to visit a parishioner in Northwest Christian Hospital.

Being newly baptized in the Spirit, I prayed intensely for the healing of this person, who was less than impressed!

I thought, what else could go wrong today? Everything I have touched so far this day has turned into utter failure!

On the way home, while waiting for a red light to change, I noticed that the car in front of me apparently had a crease in the bumper that traveled up the trunk. My eyes followed the crease, and at the very top of this crease was a bright bumper sticker, which read: "PRAISE THE LORD ANYWAY!"

For me, this was a homily etched in stone. Up to that point nothing made any sense that whole day, but suddenly this message helped me to understand that today's failures helped me to put things into perspective.

Even if I wasn't having any fun, if the Lord was being praised, that was great!

How does this work?

One day as I was praying I had a sense of an inner voice saying to me: "When you praise me for whom I am, you stand in the right relationship with me and I give you everything you need, but not everything you want!"

That made sense to me. Standing in the right relationship with Jesus!

Since that day I have seen near disasters turn into victories through praising God for who He is.

As we begin our study of praise, let us look at how the gift of praise was used to celebrate the coming of the Messiah.

We can do no better than begin with Mary's visit to Elizabeth.

When Mary entered the home of her cousin, "Elizabeth, filled with the Holy Spirit, cried out in a loud voice and said, 'Most blessed are you among women, and blessed is the fruit of your womb. And how does this happen to me, that the mother of my Lord should come to me? For at the moment the sound of your greeting reached my ears, the infant in my womb leaped for joy. Blessed are you who believed that what was spoken to you by the Lord would be fulfilled'."

Notice that Elizabeth was "filled with the Holy Spirit" and that she "cried out in a loud voice." All of you mothers here would be crying out in a loud voice if the Lord had delivered a child from your womb when you were in your eighties! She has an excuse to cry out in joy!

It is God's own Spirit that inhabits our praises. Elizabeth did not merely whisper these praises, but she "cried out in a loud voice."

The coming of the Messiah is not a routine event. This is an event that was awaited for over 1,000 years, and therefore is something worth shouting about from the top of our voices!

This is not a one-time event. Every time we advert to Christ's magnificent coming, not only in Bethlehem, but also when we take the time to reflect on the implications of His birth in us, this is a time to shout for joy for what He is doing in our midst.

That is exactly what Mary teaches us as she responds to Elizabeth's outburst of awe and wonder. She sings out:

> "My soul proclaims the greatness of the Lord,
>
> my spirit rejoices in God my Savior.
>
> For he has looked upon his handmaid's lowliness;
>
> behold, from now on will all ages call me blessed.
>
> The Mighty One has done great things for me and
>
> holy is His name."

Notice, Mary is not taking credit for the good things that are happening. She is giving all the credit to God, who is mighty and has done great things in her.

All of us can echo and re-echo Mary's praise of God every day, as we do in evening prayer.

However, we do not have to wait for evening prayer to "magnify the Lord." We can do it throughout the day, whether things are going just as we decreed, or whether nothing is going as planned. I especially encourage you to magnify the Lord when everything else is going wrong!

This is a wonderful way to enter into praising the God of Heaven who gave us the whole created universe, as well as the gift of life to recognize the beauty of His creation, but especially and above all the gift of knowing that we are all headed to one day join the Messiah and all the angels and saints in praising God.

This is a magnificent gift God has given us, the gift to praise Him for the coming of Jesus in our lives and in the lives of our families. Nothing can compare with this great gift. Even if everything else is going wrong, entering into this marvelous gift of praising God for sending us a Messiah puts all things in perspective.

I do not care how depressed or despondent you might be, simply praising God for the gift of the Messiah drives away the Evil One, as well as our discouraging thoughts, and fills our spirits with hope and confidence.

It quickly reminds us that our present discouragement is but a passing stage in the light of the glory that we can enter into by simply magnifying the Lord.

As we join Mary, we see that all the good things that happen in our lives come from His initiative. We are all headed for the kingdom of glory. Why not warm up now for the glory that is to come!

We also realize that from where these gifts come, more and more gifts are headed our way!

Let me share with you an image of where we are right now!

As we continue to live the faith, we are in a giant rocket ship, fueled by the Blood of the Lamb, headed for the heart of the Trinity.

So, to keep things in perspective, praise the Lord anyway!
It is our entertainment along the way!

Mary, Our Lady of Mount Carmel, pray for us.

Chapter Eight

The Sacrament of the Present Moment

"Therefore, I tell you, do not worry about your life... Do not worry at all about tomorrow; tomorrow will take care of itself. Sufficient for today is its own evil." (Matt 6:25-35)

It is easy to tell myself not to worry, but then I freak myself out by worrying.

I had a dear aunt, Aunt Rose, who did so much to help raise a large family. Aunt Rose loved to worry.

One day I said: "Aunt Rose, I play golf because I enjoy it."

She said: "Oh, I am glad!"

Then I said, "If you really love to worry, I would do a lot of it!"

She said: "I don't enjoy it!" I said, "I know!"

Some people worry more than others. Like my Aunt Rose, I do my share. What I needed was a concrete formula that would effectively help me to combat the compulsion of worrying or being anxious about what could happen.

I got my answer as a college seminarian seventy years ago. My older brother opened the door for me to enter the seminary by going himself. When he told me five years later that he was leaving, I was panic-stricken.

r laughed. "You are trying to take on the next
s of your life every day and no one can do that.

..... you need to do is to follow Father Cassaude's advice in *Self-Abandonment To Divine Providence.* It is called the 'Sacrament of the Present Moment.' When you arise each morning simply say to God: 'From now till noon I will embrace whatever happens to me as a manifestation of Your will.' Then renew this at noontime. In the evening as you review the day you might well say with relief: 'This morning I prepared myself for crucifixion and it did not happen!'"

This simple attitude transformed my life.

For example, during the five-minute break between college classes I was asked by a priest to get something for him from the carpentry shop. I raced down, only to discover that I had lent the key out. There was a momentary flash of anger replaced by a hearty belly laugh. "It is God's will that this door stays locked, and I am not about to open it."

When I reported back to the waiting priest, he laughed, and so did I. I had a great day!

Let us start with Jesus in the gospels. In the Gospel of John, He says: "I do only what I see the Father doing." Again, He says: "The Father is working, and I am working."

In the Garden Jesus said, "Father, thy will, not mine be done." He always experienced peace doing the Father's will.

St. Paul, in Romans 8:35-39, tells us: "Who shall separate us from the love of Christ? Shall tribulation or distress, or persecution, or famine or nakedness, or peril, or sword? ... No, in all these things we are more than conquerors through him who loved us."

"For I am sure that neither death, nor life, nor angels, nor principalities, nor things present, nor things to come, nor powers, nor height, nor depth, nor anything else in creation will be able to separate us from the love of God in Christ Jesus our Lord."

The daily practice of this habit has stood me in good stead again and again.

In our lives, God's will is everything, and doing His will brings us incredible peace!

Again and again in John's gospel, Jesus says: "I do only what I see the Father doing" and again: "The Father is working and I am working."

This enabled Him daily to adapt His plans to the circumstances before Him. For example, when He wanted to pass through Samaria on His way to Jerusalem, the Samaritans refused to let Him. He immediately decided to go around Samaria.

Even in the Garden He said: "Not my will but Thy will be done."

God uses the people who surround us, our family members, our neighbors, our business associates, and our friends, to help us make breakthroughs in holiness.

Our life is really a school of spirituality in which God is with us every moment of the day to teach us how to come closer to Him and to each other.

Our families are such a school of spirituality. Parents teach children how to be good children, and children teach parents how to be loving parents. In that sense a family is similar to a monastery.

Since a family is a school of formation, similar to a monastery, what St. John of the Cross said about brothers in the community applies also to families.

"The first precaution is to understand that you have come to the monastery so that all may fashion you and try you.

"Thus, to free yourself from imperfections and disturbances that can be engendered by the mannerism and attitudes of the religious, and draw profit from every occurrence, you should think that all in the community are artisans - as indeed they are - present there in order to prove you; that some will fashion you with words, others by deeds and others with thoughts against you, and that in all this you must be submissive as is the statue of the craftsman who molds it, to the artists who paints it, and to the gilder who embellishes it."

I had the privilege of staying with my mother for one night, a week before she passed away. I said to her: "Mom, you don't know how grateful you and Dad should be to us fifteen children who did everything to make both of you saints." She laughed because she knew that I was right.

Every individual in the family is gifted to help along in this formation process.

Certainly prayer, the family Rosary and the sacraments are vital resources to help us get along. One of the things that really work in the area where there are deep hurts is intercessory prayer for those who have hurt us.

If we can visualize ourselves as being beloved children of the Father, it goes so far to help us replace the negative image we have of ourselves.

The next step is to intercede for the person who has hurt us, wishing that our Heavenly Father would reveal to them His true image of them. When that is our prayer, we are entering into the goodness of the Father for them.

However, bottom line is that God is present to us in our presence with others, and this always makes the problems easier.

Some of you may have had to face the tragedy of a sudden death in the family, or even worse, if this was the case of suicide! This is far behind anything that you can fix.

It is in moments like this that you are called to trust. You are called to believe that God is bigger than this tragedy, and He can enable you to survive, but even more, to thrive.

God can do so much more than what we give Him credit for!

During the time of the Curé of Ars in France, there was living in Paris a saintly housewife by the name of Madame Simone. Her husband was an agnostic and wrote hateful tracts against the Church.

One day he jumped to his death. Madame Simone was crushed. She hopped a train to Ars and when she arrived, she yelled, "Where is the Curé? Where is the Curé?" They told her she had to get in line for confession and the lines were two days long! She said: "I can't wait two days!"

She went into church and silently poured out her heart at the communion rail. The Curé, in the confessional, sensed someone in church in deep turmoil. He came out of the confessional and saw the woman at the Communion rail.

He approached her and said: "Madame, your husband is not lost. He is saved!" She yelled back at him, "You don't even know him, how can you say something so hurtful?"

He responded: "I know that I don't know him, but I do know this. When you decided to hang in your living room a picture of the Sacred Heart, he did not object. God will use any good thing that we have done to save us. Your husband, between the time he jumped from the bridge and the time he hit the pavement, made a perfect act of contrition".

God is constantly calling us to trust in His will in all things.

My whole focus tonight has been to encourage you to embrace the present moment as a manifestation of God's will.

God created us in goodness, and He sustains us in the graces Christ merited for us on the cross. "My grace is sufficient for you, for strength is made perfect in weakness."

God really comes alive in my life when I humble myself and allow Him to come in and participate in my life.

When things are not going according to my plan or my expectations, I simply say: "Lord, I hope you are having fun! I am not."

That is when I praise the Lord anyway, and suddenly God's way comes to birth in my life.

Jesus tells us: "Seek first the kingdom of God and his righteousness, and all these things will be given to you besides."

Mary, Our Lady of Mount Carmel, pray for us.

Chapter Nine

16th Sunday in Ordinary Time - 2019

Genesis 18:1-10a

Colossians 1:24-28

Luke 10:38-42

God created us with abundant weakness so that we would hunger for His word!

One of the three visitors in the desert told Abraham: "I will surely return to you about this time next year, and Sarah will have a son."

Today's readings demonstrate that God created man dependent upon Him and others, so that man might cry out in desperation, hungering for the word of God! That is the profoundest hunger we experience within.

Today's first reading tells us: "The Lord appeared to Abraham by the terebinth of Mamre, as he sat in the entrance of his tent, while the day was growing hot."

God knows only too well of Abraham's spirit of hospitality in the hot desert, so He allows Abraham to see three men standing nearby.

Abraham does not know that these are three angels who appear as men. Thinking they are men in need of hospitality, "when he saw them, he ran from the entrance of the tent to greet them; and bowing to the ground, he said: 'Sir, if I may ask you this favor, please do not go on past your servant. Let some water be brought, so that you may bathe your feet, and then rest yourselves under the tree."

For starters, Abraham offers them a shade tree to protect them from the hot sun, rest for their weary bones, and water to drink and to refresh their tired and dusty feet!

He follows up with having Sarah prepare some fresh bread. He picks out a choice steer and has his servant prepare it. Abraham sets this delicious and refreshing meal before the three men who are not in need of shade, rest, food or drink. These three men graciously accept Abraham's hospitality. They thereby allow Abraham to see himself as a magnanimous man.

They then turn the table of hospitality on Abraham: "They asked Abraham, 'Where is your wife Sarah?' He replied, 'There in the tent.' One of them said, 'I will surely return to you about this time next year, and Sarah will then have a son.'"

It was only after the 90-year-old Sarah became pregnant that Abraham realized that he had just entertained three angels! Abraham had undoubtedly been proud to offer to what he thought were three needy men, the finest in desert hospitality. He then realized that he had been living in a desert of waiting for a son for roughly sixty years! It was then that Abraham realized that he, who was living in the desert of childlessness, was given the finest gift God could possibly have given him!

Today's gospel is more of the same. Now it is a woman's turn to show hospitality. We are all familiar with the story of Martha, preparing a meal for Jesus, and how she demands that God tell her sister Mary to join her!

Is Martha's hospitality really hospitality or is it a cry for human recognition? She wants recognition for what she does, whereas Mary simply offers Jesus the kind of hospitality He desires, a listening heart!

Remember Jesus once said: "Blessed are those who hear the word of God and keep it!"

There was no one who did this better than did His mother Mary. When the shepherds had visited the child in Bethlehem, "they made known the message that had been told them about this child.

"All who heard it were amazed by what had been told them by the shepherds. And Mary kept all these things, reflecting on them in her heart."

In reflecting on the things the shepherds told her, Mary was preparing her heart for the time when these passages were to unfold, especially in Christ's passion.

The greatest hospitality we can show Christ is a quiet and receptive heart in the presence of His word.

It is in this silence that He offers Himself to our hearts. It pleases Him to no end when we are receptive, because what we take in from Him in silence will be returned to Him in doing His will.

Yes, we are created in weaknesses in order that we can become pregnant with the word of God. When we become pregnant with the word of God, that word feeds us and energizes us to do the will of God.

Feast your hungry spirits on Paul's words to the Colossians in today's second reading.

"Now I rejoice in my sufferings for your sake, and in my flesh I am filling up what is lacking in the afflictions of Christ on behalf of His body, which is the Church, of which I am a minister in accordance with God's stewardship given to me to bring to completion for you the word of God, the mystery hidden from ages and from generations past."

This is a real gusher!

It was because of Paul's quiet listening that the will of God exploded in his heart so that he rejoiced in suffering for Christ so that he could fill up in his flesh "what is lacking in the afflictions of Christ on behalf of His body."

Unless one is pregnant with the word of God, one could never rejoice in suffering the way that Paul celebrates this suffering!

It is in quiet time before the word of God that the Lord enlarges our hearts to embrace the uncomfortable sufferings that come our way as gifts, enabling us to show God our great hospitality by our courageous deeds. Because Paul was so imbued with the word of God, his freely embraced suffering was not a problem but a great gift from God, the reward for obedience and generosity that flows forth from meditating on His word.

Remember, in today's gospel, Martha was seeking human consolation, while Mary was silently taking in God's will. Paul is doing the same thing. In silently meditating on God's word, both Paul and Mary experience torrents of consolations flowing from their embrace of God's will.

This hunger to embrace God's will with all of our heart, comes from first receiving this power from on high in the silent listening to His word.

How are you and I using this daily gift?

Perhaps the greatest gift we can take from this Novena is the image of Mary treasuring God's word in her heart, and then, with Mary, magnifying the Lord, for He Who is mighty is doing great things in me, and holy is His name.

This means that we need to set aside daily quiet time to relish the word that feeds our hungry spirits!

Let's take a moment of silence and ask Mary for this grace!

Mary, Our Lady of Mount Carmel, pray for us.

Novena Prayer to Our Lady of Mount Carmel

O, most beautiful flower of Mount Carmel,

Fruitful Vine, Splendor of Heaven,

Blessed Mother of the Son of God, Immaculate Virgin,

Assist me in this my necessity.

O, Star of the Sea,

Help me and show me herein

You are my Mother.

O, Holy Mary, Mother of God,

Queen of Heaven and earth,

I humbly beseech you from the bottom of my heart

To succor me in this my necessity.

There are none that can withstand your power.

O, show me herein

You are my Mother.

O, Mary conceived without sin,

Pray for us who have recourse to thee.

Sweet Mother, I place this cause in your hands.

Amen.

Auxiliary Bishop Emeritus Robert J. Hermann

Ordained a Priest of the Archdiocese of St. Louis in 1963 and ordained a Bishop in 2002.

He began his ministry in Weingarten, Missouri. He taught in the Archdiocesan high schools and taught English for twelve years at St. Louis Prep North. He also served as pastor for a total of twenty years, first at St. Andrew Parish and then at Incarnate Word Parish in Chesterfield. It was at Incarnate Word Parish that he was instrumental in starting the LIFE TEEN program. He has also had the privilege of working in the Catholic Renewal, which has impacted the lives of countless people who need this healing ministry.

After ordination to the episcopacy, he was appointed a Vicar General and Archdiocesan Administrator. In December of 2010 he became Auxiliary Bishop Emeritus.

In August of 2017, Bishop Hermann began serving as a part-time Spiritual Director at Kenrick-Glennon Seminary.

He is most grateful for the incredible opportunities God has given him to serve.